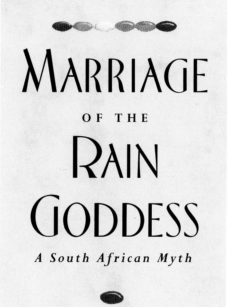

MARRIAGE
OF THE
RAIN
GODDESS

A South African Myth

To Kiki, Daniel, and Maya — *M. W.*

To my children, Jericho and Ian — *C. P.*

And to the children of the New South Africa — *M. W. and C. P.*

Barefoot Books
37 West 17th Street
4th Floor East
New York, New York 10010

First published in the United States of America in 1996 by Marlowe & Company

This edition published in 1999 by Barefoot Books, Inc.

This book is printed on 100% acid-free paper

Graphic design by Design / Section, England
Printed and bound in Singapore by Tien Wah Press (Pte) Ltd

3 5 7 9 8 6 4 2

Publisher Cataloging-in-Publication Data

Wolfson, Margaret, 1953-
    Marriage of the rain goddess : a South African myth / written by Margaret Olivia Wolfson ;
illustrated by Clifford Alexander Parms.—1st ed.
[32]p. : col. ill. ;   cm.
Summary: The rain goddess longs to find a companion to share her joy and love for the world.
But will her chosen partner be able to see beyond her appearance to the soul that lies beneath?
A haunting retelling of a traditional Zulu myth.
ISBN 1-84148-100-9
1. Zulu (African people) — Folklore. 2. Folklore — South Africa.
I. Parms, Clifford Alexander, ill. II. Title.
398.2089—dc21 1999 AC   CIP

MARRIAGE

OF THE

RAIN

GODDESS

A South African Myth

written by

MARGARET OLIVIA WOLFSON

illustrated by

CLIFFORD ALEXANDER PARMS

BAREFOOT BOOKS

This is the story of Mbaba Mwana Waresa, the rain goddess. Mbaba Mwana Waresa lived in the clouds, in a round hut made of rainbow arches. The earth people loved the rain goddess. When they heard the BOOM! BOOM! of her thunder-drum they knew the rains would come. They knew that soon bright pools of water would shine on earth, providing refreshment for birds, beasts and insects. They knew that her rains would ripen their land with pumpkins and squash, melons and berries.

Still, the rain goddess was lonely. She longed for a companion. She wanted a mate to share the joy she felt when, peeking through the clouds, she observed sea snails floating on crystal bubbles, eland and antelope drinking from pools, and crickets and frogs croaking and singing on moon-gold nights.

In search of a partner, the rain
goddess journeyed through the heavens.
But though the gods were handsome,
fearless and strong, they stirred no love in
her heart. They were too busy with their
spears and shields.

And so the rain goddess decided to seek
her husband among the mortals. She
changed herself into a shaft of sunlight
and in glittering golden beams fell to the
village below her hut. With radiant eyes,
she peered through open doorways,
watching the people as they ate and
talked, cooked and slept and polished
their earthen floors until they gleamed
like black pearls. But no man here moved
her heart.

The goddess became a cloud. She flew over swamps and hills, forests and grasslands, watching the women planting crops, men tending cattle, and the inyanga healing the sick with herbs and roots. She smiled at the boys rolling melons down the hill, trying to hit them with spears before they reached the bottom. And her heart softened at the sight of the girls, weaving love-letters from colored beads.

Finally, after many months of wandering, her eyes came to rest on a young cattle-herder named Thandiwe.

Thandiwe was returning to his kraal, singing as he went. He sang about flower-jeweled fields and bright green snakes coiled like bracelets on rocks. The beauty of his music told the goddess much about the depth of his heart. Still, he was a mortal. He must be tested. Smiling, the goddess returned to her rainbow hut, a gleaming curtain of rain falling from each footstep.

That night, Thandiwe had a dream. In this dream he saw a magical being, glistening in oil and golden bracelets, her face half-hidden by twisted leaves. She handed him a small square of colored beads.

Thandiwe knew the meaning of many of the colors. The white told him her love was pure; the brown that it was as rich as earth; and the blue that she would fly across endless skies to meet him.

The magical woman then said, "You are destined to marry Mbaba Mwana Waresa, the rain goddess. When you awake, begin building the iqati, the bridal home. When the hut is finished, stand before it. No matter what happens, wait there for your bride."

When Thandiwe awoke, he shook his head in disbelief. Resting in his hand was a love-letter of colored beads.

The next day, Thandiwe began building his bridal hut. When it was finished, he stood before it and waited.

As Thandiwe waited, the rain goddess prepared for her marriage. She shaved her head, and covered it with a ragged cloth. She removed her rainbow-colored skirt and wrapped herself in a torn zebra skin. She smeared her beautiful brown skin with ashes. Then she summoned a young girl named Nomalanga to her rainbow hut.

The goddess dressed Nomalanga in the costume of a Zulu bride. She draped coils of colored beads around the girl's neck and waist and covered her face with a veil of twisted leaves. She circled Nomalanga's wrists with gold and copper and adorned her with polished pebbles and shells. She rubbed her skin with oil until it glistened like sunlight on water. When she had finished, the goddess stepped back and smiled. Nomalanga was beautiful.

Meanwhile, Thandiwe continued to wait. "Look at the fool!" a villager shouted. "He thinks he is getting married, but no girl has been promised him. Thandiwe! You are crazier than the hyena who tries to catch the moon's reflection in its jaws!"

Suddenly, storm clouds gathered on the horizon and jagged streaks of lightning flashed across the sky.

"It's the Lightning Bird!" the villagers cried in terrified voices as they scurried for shelter. Like the others, Thandiwe was afraid. He knew the evil of the Lightning Bird. Those killed by its powerful energy were buried without ceremony. Animals struck by the Lightning Bird were not eaten. Huts touched by its talons were later destroyed — burned to the ground in great crackling fires.

Thandiwe shuddered, fear clawing at his heart. But he remained in front of the bridal hut, steadfastly awaiting the magical woman seen in his dream.

Then, as quickly as it had come, the storm passed and a rainbow slid down from the heavens.

When the rainbow touched the ground, two women stepped from the shimmering bow. Looking Thandiwe in the eye and pointing to Nomalanga, the rain goddess said, "This is the beautiful being you saw in your dream. This is your bride."

Thandiwe regarded the girl, shining like a vision. Then he looked at the woman who had spoken. She was dull and gray, her head covered in rags.

"This girl is not my bride," said Thandiwe. "You may be dressed in torn zebra skins and covered with ashes, but these things cannot conceal your splendor. In your eyes I see the bright gleam of rivers, ponds, lakes and seas. In your eyes I see the power of one who greens the earth and nourishes the crops. Such power far surpasses the charm of well-oiled skin and the jingling of bracelets and cowry shells. You are my bride. You are Mbaba Mwana Waresa, the rain goddess."

When the goddess heard these words, she knew she had chosen wisely. "Let the ceremonies begin," she said.

Soon the villagers were dancing and feasting, celebrating the marriage of Mbaba Mwana Waresa and Thandiwe. It was only when the sun dipped behind the hills and the stars sparkled, silver beads in the sky, that the festivities came to an end.

While everyone was sleeping, Mbaba Mwana Waresa and Thandiwe left the earth. Hand in hand, they journeyed to the rainbow hut, high up in the African heavens. And there they live to this very day and will always live, for Thandiwe had become a god, and like the souls of mortal men and women, gods and goddesses never die.

A F T E R W O R D

Marriage of the Rain Goddess *was inspired by a fragment of a Zulu myth of the Natal region. The author has expanded this mythic fragment by developing the story's characters and by interspersing episodes, customs and beliefs that dramatize and vivify its message. Her primary sources were* Ancient Mirrors of Womanhood *by Merlin Stone,* The Realm of the Rain Queen *by E. J. Krige and* Speaking with Beads *by Eleanor Preston Whyte.*

Of particular interest in this retelling is the role of the ucu, a Zulu term that translates as "neck ornament." One form of this multi-colored bead ornament is the Zulu "love-letter." Many ucu squares contain messages which are communicated through the symbolic use of color and design. Young Zulu women weave and give these "love-letters" to young men, so these necklaces are associated with courtship.

In the spirit of the myth's timeless nature, Clifford Parms has chosen to mix more modern styles of traditional clothing and beadwork with older designs and colors. Although creative license has been taken in bringing together clothing and beadwork of diverse regions, the majority of images represented in this work are associated with the Zulu culture. The English meaning of the Zulu names are: Mother of the Rains (Mbaba Mwana Waresa, pronounced Ma-baba Ma-wana Wa-re-sa); sunny or sunlight (Nomalanga, pronounced No-ma lan-ga) and beloved (Thandiwe, pronounced Tan-dee-way).

BAREFOOT BOOKS publishes high-quality picture books for
children of all ages and specializes in the work of artists and writers from
many cultures. If you have enjoyed this book and would like to receive a copy of
our current catalog, please contact our New York office —
Barefoot Books Inc., 37 West 17th Street, 4th Floor East, New York, New York 10010
e-mail: ussales@barefoot-books.com   website: www.barefoot-books.com